Contemporary Hispanic Americans

JOSÉ CANSECO

BY
BETTINA LING

RSVP

RAINTREE
STECK-VAUGHN
PUBLISHERS
The Steck-Vaughn Company

Austin, Texas

Published by Raintree Steck-Vaughn, an imprint of Steck-Vaughn Company.
Produced by Mega-Books, Inc.
Design and Art Direction by Michaelis/Carpelis Design Associates
Cover photo: Focus on Sports

Library of Congress Cataloging-in-Publication Data
Ling, Bettina.
    José Canseco/by Bettina Ling.
        p. cm. — (Contemporary Hispanic Americans)
    Includes bibliographical references and index.
    Summary: A biography of José Canseco, the major league baseball player who made a comeback despite serious injury, being traded by the Oakland Athletics, divorce, and depression.
    ISBN 0-8172-3983-9 (Hardcover)
    ISBN 0-8114-9790-9 (Softcover)
    1. Canseco, José, 1964-   —Juvenile literature. 2. Baseball players—United States—Biography—Juvenile literature. [1. Canseco, José, 1964-   . 2. Baseball players. 3. Cuban Americans—Biography.]
    I. Title. II. Series.
GV865.C313L56 1995
796.357'092—dc20   95-19551
[B]   CIP
                                                                                                   AC

Printed and bound in the United States.

1 2 3 4 5 6 7 8 9 LB 99 98 97 96 95

Photo credits: Focus On Sports: pp. 4, 7, 14, 18, 20, 24, 29, 30, 33, 35, 36, 39, 43, 44; UPI/Bettmann: pp. 8, 11, 12, 23; Reuters/Bettmann: pp. 26, 40; Bryan Yablonsky/DUOMO: p. 17.

Contents

Chapter One

40–40

This could be the moment José Canseco had hoped for all season. He waited on first base as his teammate, Mark McGwire, stepped up to bat. Their baseball team, the Oakland Athletics, was playing the Milwaukee Brewers at Milwaukee's County Stadium. In the first inning of the game, José had singled and stolen second base—his 39th stolen base of the season. Now, in the fifth inning, José's **bunt** had just put him on first base.

The date was September 23, 1988. Five days earlier, José had hit his 40th home run of the season in a game between the Oakland Athletics and the Kansas City Royals. If he could steal his 40th base in today's game, the 24-year-old slugger would make baseball

By the time he was 24 years old, José Canseco had set new records and become a baseball superstar.

history. He would enter the record books as the first player in the 112-year history of the major leagues to hit 40 home runs and steal 40 bases in the same season. (The closest any other player had come to getting 40-40 in one season had been Bobby Bonds; he had 39 homers and 43 stolen bases in the 1973 season while he played for the San Francisco Giants.)

José had first talked about reaching the 40-40 record during spring training, back in April. But he had played in the major leagues for only three seasons, and many people did not believe he could do it. José worked very hard to prove them wrong. By August, he reached the 30-30 mark, becoming one of only 11 players in baseball history to accomplish this record. Now his 40-40 moment was finally here.

José stood ready. The baseball fans watched in excited anticipation. Milwaukee Brewers pitcher Juan Nieves wound up to pitch to Mark McGwire. But on the first pitch, José did not leave first base. His legs felt frozen. The tension was too great, the expectations too high. Could he do this? Before the second pitch, he said to himself, "If I'm going to do it, let's do it now."

On the second pitch, José took off from first base and sped toward second. The catcher threw to the second baseman, but he was too late. José slid safely into second base before the catch and tag. His 40th base was stolen! José Canseco was the "40-40 man"!

The game stopped, and the crowd in the stadium cheered. José's fellow teammates applauded. He stood

José Canseco became the first player in baseball history to hit forty home runs and steal forty bases in one season.

up, dusted himself off, and then bent down and pulled second base out of the ground. José raised it over his head in triumph. The feeling of success was wonderful! By the time the game was over, José also had his 41st home run. The Oakland Athletics won by a 9-8 score over Milwaukee.

The Milwaukee game confirmed José Canseco's position as one of major league baseball's fastest-rising stars. In 1986, his first full year in the major leagues, he had been named Rookie of the Year. Now, with his 40-40 triumph, the 1988 season seemed to hold just as much promise. He had the most home runs of any player in the major leagues for the year. He was first in **RBIs** and second in runs scored. He also had the league's highest **batting average**.

By the time the 1988 season ended, José Canseco had led his team to its first American League **pennant** since 1981. Now they had the chance to play in the World Series against the Los Angeles Dodgers. He would be voted the Associated Press Player of the Year, elected by a panel of sportswriters and broadcasters. In addition, he would be named the American League's Most Valuable Player (MVP). José would

José celebrates a seventh-inning home run in a 1988 game against Boston. By the end, José would become the American League's MVP.

become only the seventh player in history, and the first in 15 years, to be elected MVP by unanimous vote. What's more, his baseball contract for the next season with the Oakland A's would make him a millionaire. His fabulous success seemed like it could go on forever.

Only one thing kept the year from being perfect— the Oakland Athletics lost the World Series to the Dodgers. For José, the team's surprising defeat was a shadow on an otherwise bright year. It foretold the difficulties and disappointments that were to come.

José Canseco was to discover that he would need more than his talent to be considered a great baseball player. Being a star would carry him to the greatest highs and the deepest lows of his life.

Chapter Two

FROM CUBA TO MIAMI

José Canseco, Jr., and his twin brother Osvaldo (Ozzie) were born in Havana, Cuba, on July 2, 1964. Their parents, José, Sr., and Barbara, already had a daughter named Teresa. Life was very hard at that time for the Canseco (the name is pronounced Can-SAY-ko) family. It had not always been this way. During the 1950s, José, Sr., was an executive with an oil company, and the family had lived a comfortable life.

In 1959, the Communist leader Fidel Castro took control of the Cuban government, and life in Cuba changed for its citizens. The new Cuban government claimed the property of many of the wealthier people in Cuba. José Canseco, Sr., lost his house and his car. He also lost his job. Then he made a living by giving English lessons at his home for $15 a month. By the time the boys were born, the Cansecos had applied to the Cuban government for visas needed to emigrate to the United States.

After leaving Cuba, the Cansecos made their new home in Miami. Shown here is a main street in Miami Beach in 1962, shortly before the Canseco family arrived.

In 1965, the Cansecos finally received permission to leave Cuba. They left with only fifty dollars and no job prospects in the United States. José and Ozzie were just nine months old. For the next ten years, they lived in Miami with José, Sr.'s, sister. José, Sr., worked at two jobs—one at a gas station during the day and another as a night security guard.

Life in America was made even more difficult by Barbara Canseco's fragile health. After she had given birth to José and Ozzie in Cuba, Barbara needed a blood transfusion. The blood she was given was infected. Barbara Canseco was never fully well again.

Even with José, Sr., working long hours and Barbara's ill health, there were plenty of good times for the Canseco children. José and Ozzie were extremely close, and they loved playing together. Their mother enjoyed caring for her home and family. She liked to cook and laugh with her children. José, Sr., was a tough, but loving parent. He led a very strict life, and expected his children to do the same. Neither of the elder Cansecos smoked or drank.

When the Canseco twins were ten years old, their

José Canseco has remained close to his family and to his roots in the Miami Cuban-American community. Here, he visits his father's home in 1986.

father found work as a manager for an oil company. He had saved money from the two jobs he had worked at for almost a decade. Now he bought a home for his family in the Westchester section of Miami.

Life in this part of Miami was comfortable for José and his family. The area had a largely Hispanic-American population. Shop owners spoke Spanish to their customers. In restaurants the sound of Latin music could be heard playing in the background. Neighbors and business owners usually knew each other well. After school and on weekends, the neighborhood children would play baseball or swim at the community pool. Two of these childhood friends, Rafael Palmiero and Danny Tartabull, also grew up to become major league baseball players.

When José played baseball as a child, he was not known as a great player. He didn't even show that much interest in the game. Both José and Ozzie were skinny children who studied more than they played sports. Thanks to their parents' emphasis on education, José and Ozzie were straight-A students from grade school through junior high. They did not play organized sports until they were 12 years old.

However, José, Sr., expected his children to be the best at whatever they did. After all, José, Sr., himself came to America with only fifty dollars in his pocket and built his family's life into a success. So when José and Ozzie started playing baseball in high school, José, Sr., would reward the boys with five dollars for every

As boys, José and Ozzie Canseco were thin and studious. No one guessed that both brothers would one day end up playing professional ball.

home run they hit. He continued to do this through-out their early years in the major leagues.

José and Ozzie attended Coral Park High School in Miami. José played third base, and Ozzie pitched on the high school team. While Ozzie was considered an excellent player, José was thought to be only moderately good. It would be several years before his true talent would appear.

Three

FROM MINOR TO MAJOR

It was Ozzie who made the Coral Park varsity team first. He joined the team during his junior year, while José had to wait until his senior year to make the cut. José was still skinny then. He stood about six feet tall and weighed between 155 and 165. "I think I was just a late bloomer," José says about his high school baseball years.

While playing on the varsity team, José began to improve his game. He had a good batting year, hitting for a .400 average. A baseball scout for the Oakland Athletics named Camilio Pascual noticed José's batting potential during that senior year. Camilio was also Cuban-born and had been a pitcher in the major leagues for 18 years before becoming a scout. Baseball scouts travel around the country looking for young players in order to find new talent for the major league teams.

Camilio Pascual spotted something in José's hitting

that the scouts from the other teams did not see. No other scout listed him as a good prospect for playing major league baseball. Camilio convinced the Oakland A's management to take a chance on José and offer him a contract to play ball for their team.

This was a wonderful opportunity for José Canseco. During his high school years his studies had taken a backseat to baseball and to one of José's newest passions, fast cars. It was exciting that a scout from a major league baseball team thought he had a future as a professional ball player.

There was more exciting news for the Canseco family. Ozzie was also offered a contract with a major league team, the New York Yankees. The brothers signed with their teams after they graduated from high school in 1982. José was sent to play for one of the Oakland A's rookie league teams.

Professional baseball is made up of different levels of leagues. The highest level are the major league teams. The lower levels are called the minor league teams. When major league teams sign up new players, they are usually sent to play in the minor leagues to get more experience and training.

The minor leagues are made up of four levels, or classes. Rookie league farm teams are the lowest class. The next level are the Class A teams, then Class AA. Class AAA are the highest level. It is from the Class AAA teams that players "graduate," when their ability improves, to playing in the major league games.

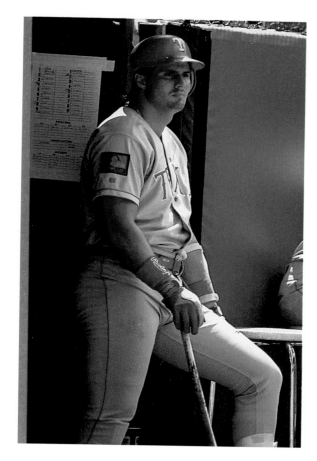

At six feet, three inches and 230 pounds, José Canseco is far from the skinny boy who played for his high school team.

José Canseco's first season on the rookie team was a struggle for him. He did not hit well. By the next season, he had sprouted up to six feet, three inches and been introduced to weight training. He was soon moved from the rookie team to the Class A Northwest League and was moved from third base to play the outfield. His playing improved, even though he lead the league in strikeouts. José then moved up to the Huntsville, Alabama, Stars, a Class AA team in the

A scout for the Oakland Athletics was the first to notice something special in José's hitting. One day, the whole world would see it, too!

Southern League. But something was still missing. José did not yet have a real commitment to the game.

It was during this period, in 1984, that a tragedy changed José's life. His mother, Barbara, was admitted to the hospital one Friday with bad headaches. By the next Monday she had died from a blood clot in her brain. Teresa Canseco called her two brothers. José was devastated by his mother's unexpected death. "It was like a jolt to me," he said.

Barbara Canseco's death made her son think about what was important in life. He realized that he wasn't fully dedicating himself to baseball. He had to make a true commitment. José decided to try and play as well as he could in memory of his mother.

José doubled his workouts with the weights, and developed a healthy diet. In the next year, he added 35 pounds of muscle and power to his body. Yet his batting did not improve. José still felt grief and anger over his mother's death, and this was affecting his play. Not being able to concentrate well, he struck out a lot.

José saw that because he was trying so hard to improve his game, he was not enjoying baseball. He decided to still work hard but have more fun with his game. He also learned how to live with his sadness over his mother's death. He never stopped missing her. Finally, he managed to recover from his shock and pain.

At last, José's batting began to improve. He changed the way he stood when he was at bat. With his new stance, relaxed attitude, and powerful muscles, José could now slam balls out of Huntsville's Joe Davis Stadium. His hits were so long that they went over the back stadium wall and onto the street behind it. This street got the unofficial nickname of "José Parkway." He hit 25 home runs in 58 games.

By the end of his season with Huntsville, José had a .318 batting average. Although he had missed 22

By 1985, José Canseco's power hitting had earned him a place on the Oakland A's major league team.

games when he was out with a broken hand, he was still named the Southern League's MVP.

In 1985, José went on to the Class AAA Tacoma Tigers, the Tacoma, Washington, team in the Pacific Coast League. There, he continued his remarkable power hitting. José became the first player in 26 years to hit a ball out of Tacoma's Cheney Stadium. He was starting to make a name for himself in the game.

José "graduated" from the Class AAA leagues to the major leagues in the fall of 1985. He and the rest of his family were excited and happy. José Canseco's hard work was paying off. He would finally be playing on the major league team of the Oakland Athletics.

Chapter Four

THE OAKLAND A'S AND STARDOM

José played left field for the Oakland A's during the fall of 1985, and he played well. In one week, he had a terrific .491 batting average with four home runs and was named the American League Player of the Week.

During the next year, his first full season as a major league player, José had to adapt to many changes. At spring training in April 1986, his powerful hitting was causing a stir with fans and the press. Suddenly the media spotlight focused on José and his batting. Reporters from newspapers and magazines singled José out for questions after the games. He found himself uncomfortable answering questions, which were sometimes about his personal life. He was also shy around his teammates. Some of the players and reporters accused him of being distant and moody.

Then, after the season began, José suffered a slump. His inexperience and immaturity as a major league player showed. José struck out often. In early summer he began a particularly difficult period of hitless games. In 40 times at bat he did not get a single hit.

Finally, José settled down and began to turn things around. In August he broke his hitless streak and slump with a game-winning hit in a game against the Yankees. José's playing and batting for the rest of the year were tremendous. He finished his season by hitting 33 home runs and driving in 117 runs. The year ended with a bang when José was named the American League Rookie of the Year by the Baseball Writers Association of America.

Off the field, this Rookie of the Year still liked fast cars. José would eventually own many Porsches, Ferraris, and Jaguars. José also liked listening to music and playing a little basketball with a small group of friends. He had a girlfriend named Esther Haddad, whom he had met at a Miami health club. Esther, a former beauty queen, was also Cuban American. José tried to see her whenever he could.

By his second season with Oakland, in 1987, José started to have more fun and make friends with some of his fellow players, like Reggie Jackson and Mark McGwire. Yet José's second major league baseball season was not quite as successful as the first. He brought his strike out record down from 175 in the 1986 season to 157 in the 1987 season, but his batting average was only .257.

José Canseco was still a rising star in the baseball world. This continued to bring him attention, some of

José Canseco joins Willie Mays at the 1986 "old-timers" game between the A's and the San Francisco Giants. Later that year, José would be named the American League's Rookie of the Year.

it unwanted. When José left the players' entrance at the stadium, some fans pushed to get near him or tore his clothes. He did not know how to handle this kind of attention. It became very difficult to go out to public places. Everywhere he went, people showered José with compliments, telling him how great he was. His salary jumped from $65,000 in 1986 to $350,000 in 1988. These were all exciting parts of his new life as a sports star. But it was hard for the young player not to let all the attention go to his head.

José's brother, Ozzie, was now also an Oakland A, but he was still playing in the minor leagues. He had played with the Yankees for a few years, and he came to the A's in 1986. It was hard for Ozzie, having such a famous brother. People constantly compared them. Both brothers were impatient for Ozzie to move up to the majors, so they could play on the same team.

The year 1988 started strong, with José in great shape, hitting better than ever. In spring training he talked to reporters about his confidence in his playing abilities for the new year. He felt he was playing an all-around better game now. José mentioned his goal of

José with Oakland A's teammate Mark McGwire.

trying to achieve 40 home runs and 40 stolen bases in one season. Most of the reporters laughed, thinking he could not do something so impressive.

When José finally stole his 40th base on that September night, he felt more relieved than elated. He was afraid the season might have ended without this accomplishment. Then he would have looked foolish with all of his big talk about 40-40! After pulling up the second base he stole for his 40th steal, José took it home. He kept it, along with the spike shoes and uniform he wore, the bat that he hit the 40th home run with, and the ball he hit for that home run.

The Oakland A's went on to win the American League pennant and play the Dodgers in the World Series. Although José hit a **grand slam** in the first game, he went 0 for 18 the rest of the series. The Dodgers beat the Oakland A's with some spectacular playing. The loss of the World Series was a big disappointment to José and his teammates. It was the one defeat in an otherwise winning year.

José also had another special moment in 1988. At the end of October, he married his girlfriend, Esther, in a simple, private ceremony. A week later they had a lavish wedding and reception with three hundred family members and friends.

José was on his honeymoon in Hawaii when the phone rang in his hotel room. He picked it up and was given the news that he had been named, by unanimous vote, the American League's Most Valuable

José Canseco and his wife, Esther, two years after their 1988 marriage.

Player. "I'm really surprised," he told reporters. "Winning by a unanimous vote was really exciting."

José's father, brother, family, and friends were overjoyed. José, Sr., said he was so proud of his son, that he felt like "he was walking on a cloud." The Cuban community in the Westchester section of Miami was also very proud of their hometown boy.

For José Canseco, 1988 was a year to remember. He would need all these good memories to help him through the difficult times that lay ahead.

Five

STRIKING OUT

By 1992, José Canseco, the superstar slugger, found himself unhappy, in trouble with the law, and wearing a new uniform. Just before midnight on August 31 of that year, José was suddenly and unexpectedly traded by the Oakland A's to the Texas Rangers in exchange for three players. How did he come to this point, less than four years after his fantastic season of 1988?

A number of events had contributed to the soured relationship between José and the A's. Some trouble had begun during his winning 1988 year. Unfounded rumors circulated in the press about José using drugs called steroids to build up his muscles. Another problem had been his fellow players. Some of them did not like their superstar teammate. At times, José seemed boastful about his talents as a ballplayer. His lateness for practices and his no-shows at important team functions did not help to win him new friends among his teammates.

During the beginning of 1989, there were more incidents that continued to damage José's reputation, both with the public and the A's organization. He was accused of missing a parade in Miami that was held in his honor after the World Series. What made this even more upsetting was that the parade was put on by his fellow Hispanic Americans.

José did not show up for another Miami event, a softball home run contest. He failed to make several appearances at autograph and baseball card shows. One promoter of a baseball card show sued José for not appearing at his show. Some fans thought that he had become arrogant and selfish. He seemed to have forgotten the very people who filled the baseball stadium bleachers to watch him play.

José also opened up a 900 phone number that charged fans money to hear details about his personal life. People called him greedy and self-centered for opening this phone line, even though José said half of the money he made went to charity.

In February 1989, he was stopped for speeding while driving his red customized Jaguar. The police clocked his car going at such a fast speed that José was charged with reckless driving. In March, he collected another four tickets with the same car. As a child, José had always loved speed—fast cars, boats, anything. Now, he still seemed to be acting like that little boy, and it was dangerous!

One of the worst incidents occurred in April. José

Beginning in 1988, José Canseco faced more and more problems on and off the field.

was arrested for possession of a loaded gun. The police found the gun on the floor of his parked car, while José and his wife were at the University of California at San Francisco. He said he was carrying the gun for protection. José went to court and was given three years probation. The judge ordered him to perform eighty hours of community service in hospitals. He also agreed to destroy his gun.

To add to his problems, José injured his wrist at the start of the 1989 season. During spring training he felt something pop in his left hand. The injury was serious enough that on May 10, he underwent surgery on the hand. Things seem to be going from bad to worse for this star player. Somehow, José was still able to play great baseball. When his hand healed and he returned to the game in the summer, he continued to hit massive home runs and rack up many RBIs.

By the fall, the superior playing of the Oakland A's had earned them another trip to the World Series. This time they were playing against a fellow team from the San Francisco Bay area, the San Francisco

Crowds gather at Game 3 of the 1989 World Series between San Francisco and Oakland. A major earthquake would hit the area during the game, but the A's would go on to sweep the series.

Giants. The 1989 Series was a series to remember, in more ways than one!

The beginning of Game 3 was disrupted by a powerful earthquake that hit the San Francisco Bay area. The World Series was delayed for ten days as the Bay area tried to recover from the major destruction the earthquake had caused. San Francisco's Candlestick Park had to be inspected, to make sure the stadium had not suffered damage that would make it unsafe.

When the series resumed, the Oakland A's, who had been leading two games to zero, swept the series by winning the next two games. It was the first series sweep since 1976. But José did not attend the White House ceremony honoring his team as World Series champs, adding another minus to his already negative image. He also failed to show up for the victory rally staged by the Oakland fans.

His status as a baseball superstar meant that José was now representing not just himself. He stood for his team, the cities of Oakland and Miami, and the Cuban people, as well. This was a heavy responsibility for a 25-year-old player. His personal life was no longer his own. Everything he did and said was thrown into the glare of the media spotlight.

The press reported constantly on the negative aspects of José's life. They did not give as much publicity to the positive things he did. José donated his time and money to the Miami Youth Club. He was also deeply involved with a group called the Make-A-

Wish Foundation, an organization that fulfills the fantasies of dying children. José attended charity events and signed hundreds of autographs for free, even though his autograph on a baseball card sold for over twenty dollars. Once, to help raise money for a paralyzed child, José signed autographs for four and a half hours. Another time he paid for a boy with leukemia to come and watch spring training. These were just some of the many good things José did.

During the 1990 season, personal difficulties and controversy continued to plague José. Back and wrist problems kept him out of many games. The A's made it to another World Series in the fall. However, this series would not be a repeat of the win in 1989. The A's lost in a four-game sweep by the Cincinnati Reds. For José, it was a particularly unpleasant series. He was accused of personally helping to lose Game 2. His bad play on a Cincinnati line drive had turned the hit into an eighth-inning triple. The A's manager had benched him in Game 4, and José did not play at all.

José did manage to set records in baseball that season, in spite of his injuries. In June, José signed a five-year contract with the A's for $23.5 million dollars. This made him the highest paid player in baseball. José's new contract, however, didn't improve his poor reputation. In 1991, his 200th career home run almost went unnoticed as the negative stories about him grew. He was left off the All-Star team. By 1992, many of the fans had turned against José. Taunts,

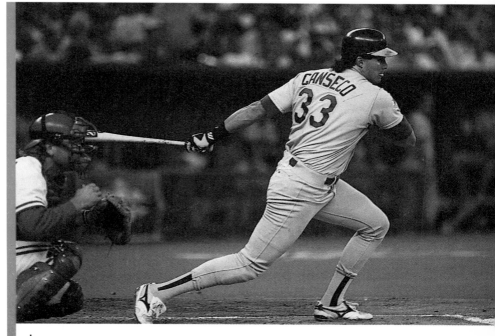

In the 1990 World Series, it was a Cincinnati sweep against Oakland. José Canseco's playing, and his reputation, were suffering.

boos, and jeers were directed at him during games.

José's life was spiraling out of control. As 1992 came to a close, he was arrested two more times— once for ramming his wife's car with his own car, and another time for punching a man in a dance club. In the summer, Hurricane Andrew slammed across Florida's southern coast. José's Miami home suffered major damage. With his back still causing him pain, his playing declined. In November his rocky marriage finally came to an end, with his wife filing for divorce. By then José had also worn out his welcome in

Oakland. He had been traded to the Texas Rangers.

In the meantime, Ozzie Canseco was having some troubles of his own, but they were all on the field. For a brief time in early July 1990, Ozzie and José had actually played together for the Oakland A's major league team. But by the end of that month, Ozzie was sent back to the minors. He left the A's in 1991 to play in the Japanese minor leagues. In 1993, he joined the St. Louis Cardinals, where he still played in the minors. By the end of 1993, he felt he would never move up to the major leagues, so he announced his retirement from baseball.

During his first full season playing with the Texas Rangers, José Canseco nearly ended his career as well. The season started out promising, with José getting his 1,000th career hit. But the tide turned against him again. In a late spring game against the Cleveland Indians, José fumbled a catch on a fly ball hit by Indians player Carlos Martinez. Aided by a bounce off José's head, the ball went over the right field wall to give Cleveland a home run. The incident made José the subject of jokes in the baseball world. Then, José made a mistake in another game. It was a mistake he will never forget.

José had done some pitching in high school and in the minor leagues. He really wanted to try pitching in the majors. He had been practicing during the year and finally Rangers manager Kevin Kennedy allowed José to pitch the eighth inning in a game against the

Texas Rangers manager Kevin Kennedy.

Boston Red Sox. José's debut as a pitcher was not remarkable. He threw 12 strikes and 21 balls, and allowed 3 runs on 2 hits. What's worse, he injured his arm during the game.

On his second pitch, José felt a sharp pain in his arm. He ignored it and continued to pitch for the rest of the game. This proved to be a very big mistake. A few days later, the arm was still sore. When doctors examined it, they discovered that José had torn a ligament in his elbow. The injury was so serious that José underwent surgery to have it repaired. He was out for the rest of the season.

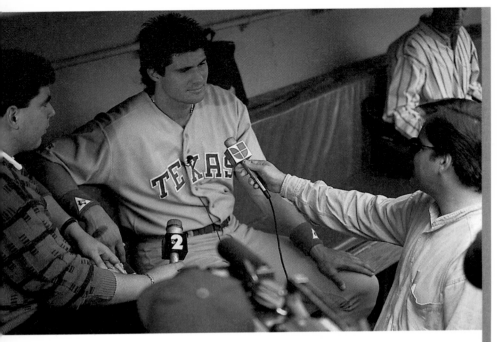

José speaks to the press during his first full season with the Texas Rangers. An injury during this season nearly ended his baseball career.

With José's season over, many people were saying his career as a baseball player was over as well. José Canseco's greatest playing strength was his powerful hitting. The serious injury to his arm seemed to indicate that he might never be able to hit well again.

Chapter **Six**

COMEBACK TRAIL

The bottom had fallen out of José Canseco's world. He had been injured, traded, and divorced. Life was at a low point for this talented ballplayer. The fans, press, and baseball world declared him finished.

José was especially troubled by his failed marriage. He went into a deep depression over this. His sadness about the divorce affected everything. He had lost a sense of who he was, so much so that he watched videotapes of old games to remind himself of the player he had been. In 1993, José started to see a special counselor, called a psychotherapist, to talk about his problems. A psychotherapist helps people work out their mental or emotional difficulties.

With help from his psychotherapist, José Canseco began to fight his way out of his deep sadness. He finally understood what had brought him to such a low period in his life, and how he had contributed to his problems. He was determined to put his mistakes behind him and remake his life. José learned to relax more and stop worrying so much about what he had to prove to the baseball world.

José made a renewed commitment to baseball. After the surgery on his elbow, he hired a physical therapist and special trainers to help him rebuild his arm. He worked with a pitching coach to improve his throwing from the outfield and a track coach to build his leg strength so he could run faster.

During the 1994 year, José said, "I'm trying to look forward now, because that's the most positive thing I can do." The new José began to love the baseball crowds again. His relations with the news media improved. He had a better relationship with his Texas Rangers teammates than he had with team members in Oakland.

José Canseco's batting power began to return, and it was stronger than ever. During his rebuilding program, José found that he wasn't swinging the bat the way he used to because he had developed some bad habits when he threw. He found a better way to throw, and he was able to return to his quick swing from his early years of play.

So that his arm could have a chance to heal, the Rangers kept him out of playing in the outfield. Instead, he became a **designated hitter**.

José's hitting comeback in 1994 was interrupted by a baseball strike by the players against the team owners during the late summer. The season ended

A powerful, confident José Canseco returned to playing as a designated hitter for Texas in 1994.

with no more games being played until the players and owners could work out their differences.

With time off from baseball, José Canseco turned his attention to helping others. After Hurricane

Andrew in 1992, he had raised funds for the storm's victims. Now, in the fall of 1994, he helped the Cuban families who were packed into camps at the United States Naval Base at Guantánamo Bay, Cuba.

In August, Cuban leader Fidel Castro had changed his policy about not allowing people to emigrate to the United States. Thousands of people left Cuba for this country, trying to escape their difficult lives in Cuba. Unfortunately, most of them arrived at one time. The United States made them wait in navy camps at Guantánamo Bay while their requests for permission to live in the United States were processed. Many families had lived in these camps for months.

José saw pictures of the hundreds of children in the

Watched by their mothers, two children play beside barbed wire in a camp for Cuban refugees. José Canseco visited these camps in 1994.

camps. He was touched by their terrible situation. José flew to Guantánamo Bay and delivered toys and hope to the children and their families.

Baseball fans in Cuba follow José's career as closely as fans in the United States. His visit to the camps meant a great deal to the Cubans being held there. The trip affected José deeply. "I've always felt a special bond toward Cuba," he said. "After seeing this, I feel a stronger bond."

During the Christmas season, José also made visits to Miami's Children's Hospital to give away toys. He stayed to play with the sick children long after the newspeople who had accompanied him had left.

José hopes one day to marry again, because he wants very much to have children. He has matured and learned from his mistakes. He continues to learn how to handle his fame. The "new" José has a positive outlook on life.

In addition to a new outlook on life, José Canseco has a new team. At the end of 1994, he was traded to the Boston Red Sox. Unlike his trade to the Texas Rangers, this trade is one José knew about. He is happy and excited about the chance to play for the Red Sox, especially since he is playing for manager Kevin Kennedy. It was Kennedy who managed the Texas Rangers when José played for that team. He also enjoys playing in Fenway Park, which is one of the oldest major league baseball parks, and also the smallest. When José played with his previous teams in games against the Red Sox there, he hit some monster home runs. Jose hopes to hit many more homers out of this ballpark.

José Canseco's life is quieter now. He does not drive fast cars anymore. They have caused him too much trouble! He stays in shape by playing softball in Florida. He has started a new venture as the owner of a sports management business. José also spends a lot of time these days in his new home in the Miami suburb of Weston. The house is very big, with seven bedrooms, a swimming pool, a gym, and a lake. He wanted a large home where he could enjoy his privacy with his family and friends, and showcase his collection of Asian art. When he is there with his family, he gets the chance to indulge in some of his favorite Cuban and Italian foods. José especially likes arroz con pollo, a Cuban rice and chicken dish, and manicotti, an Italian pasta dish.

When he's at home, José also spends time with his many different pets. He has always loved animals, and over the years he has owned a number of dogs, cats, and rare tortoises. Today, he has added tropical fish and exotic birds to his household. Besides caring for his pets, José also likes to use his free time to read science fiction novels, watch old comedy shows on television, and view movies on videotape.

José Canseco is happy to be playing for the Boston Red Sox in Fenway Park.

After several rough years in his professional and personal life, José Canseco is making a successful comeback.

José is not the only Canseco who seems to be enjoying his life again. Ozzie is on a "comeback" of his own. He is back in uniform playing with the Milwaukee Brewers on their Class AAA team, the Denver Zephyrs. He will continue to try for his own dream of making it to the major leagues.

The two nearly identical brothers are still very close. They talk on the phone about once a week and try to help each other as much as they can. Ozzie believes that his brother has what it takes to make the Baseball Hall of Fame someday. He tells the story of the time he saw José hit a ball that went up and over the centerfield fence of a high school stadium. The ball carried over the sidewalk on the other side of the fence, past the lawn, over the street, past more lawn, and past another sidewalk, and landed on the roof of a house. Ozzie estimates that the ball must have gone over 600 feet. That is Hall of Fame hitting!

After pulling himself back from the brink of disaster, José Canseco is once again ready to win. In 1994, he was only thirty years old. With new records to set, this talented Cuban American should have many years left to become one of the best players in the history of baseball.

Important Dates

1964   Born in Havana, Cuba, on July 2.

1965   Family emigrates to the United States and settles in Miami, Florida.

1982   Signs with the Oakland Athletics. Begins to play in the minor leagues.

1985   Moves up to the Oakland A's major league team.

1986   Named American League Rookie of the Year.

1988   Becomes the first player in major league history to record forty home runs and forty stolen bases in the same season. Marries Esther Haddad. Named the American League's Most Valuable Player.

1989   Oakland A's beat the San Francisco Giants in the World Series, which is interrupted by an earthquake.

1990   Signs a five-year, $23.5 million contract with the A's.

1991   Gets his 200th career home run.

1992   Divorced from Esther Haddad Canseco. Traded to the Texas Rangers team.

1993   Gets his 1,000th career hit. Major injury to arm ends playing for the rest of the season.

1994   Begins to play with Texas Rangers as a designated hitter. Later traded to the Boston Red Sox.

Glossary

batting average A percentage that is based on 1.000. To figure out an average, divide the number of times a person gets a hit by the number of times the person comes to bat. Then carry the result out to three decimal points. A .300 average means a batter came to the plate ten times and got three hits.

bunt A hit where the batter taps the ball lightly, without swinging, so that the ball rolls slowly in front of the infielders.

designated hitter A player who bats in place of the pitcher, and does not play a position on the field.

grand slam A home run hit while the bases are loaded.

pennant A flag that signifies the championship in the league, specifically in a professional baseball league.

RBIs Runs batted in. An RBI gives the player credit for driving in a run as a result of a hit, a base on balls, a sacrifice fly ball, or being hit by a pitch.

Bibliography

Cohen, Eliot, editor. *My Greatest Day in Baseball*. New York: Simon & Schuster, 1991.

Grenquist, Barbara. *Cubans* (Recent American Immigrants Series). New York: Franklin Watts, 1990.

Sullivan, George. *Sluggers: Twenty-Seven of Baseball's Greatest*. New York: Atheneum, 1991.

Index

DATE DUE

921
CAN

Ling, Bettina.

Jose Canseco